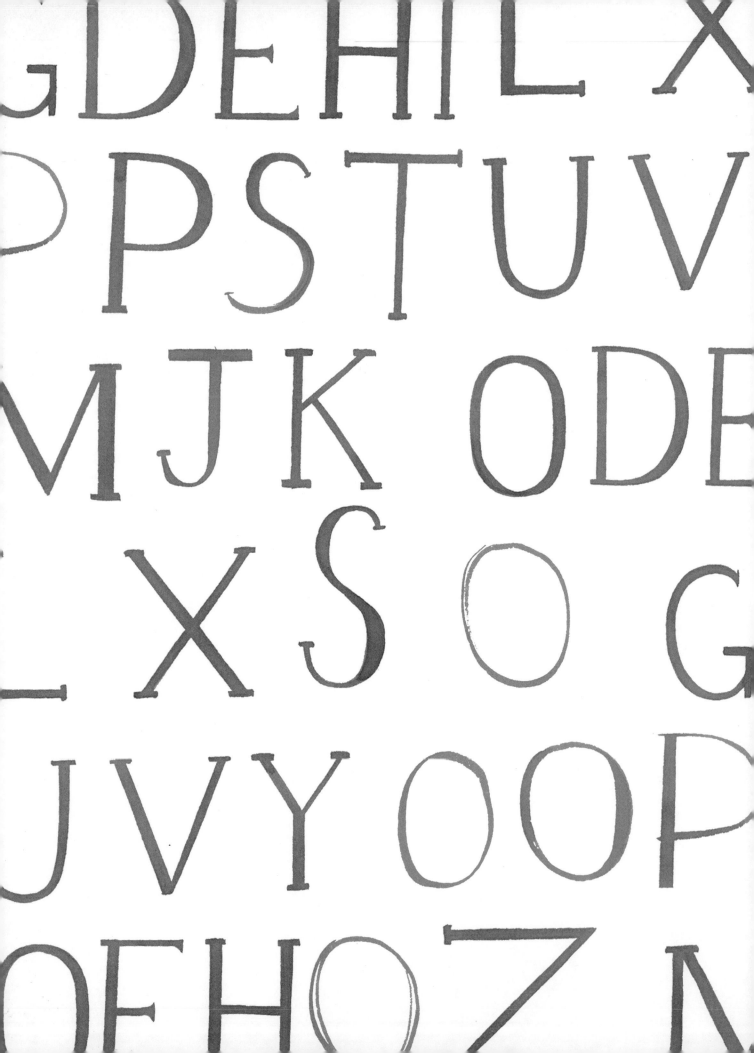

Ox, House, Stick

The History of Our Alphabet

Alphabet

Ox, House, Stick

The History of Our Alphabet

Don Robb

Illustrated by Anne Smith

COUNTY LIBRARY TILLAMOOK, ORE
DISCARD

Charlesbridge

How Do People Communicate?

Human beings have been on this planet for a long time—thousands and thousands of years, in fact. And from the very beginning, people have needed to talk to one another.

Sometimes we can talk without making a sound. We can use facial expressions, gestures, or both. But the most important way that human beings communicate with each other is through language.

Originally all language was oral: people simply spoke to one another. But spoken language doesn't let you keep a record of what was said, and it doesn't let you talk to people who are far away. So eventually, people developed written language, which lets you do both.

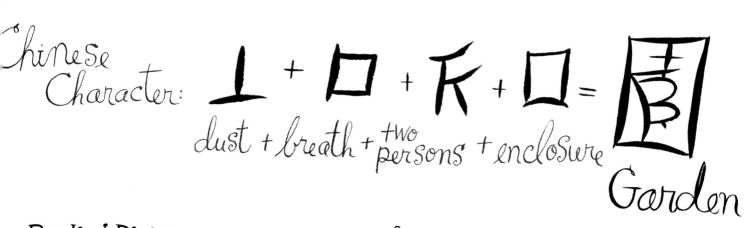

Chinese Character: 圥 + 口 + 尔 + 口 = 圌
dust + breath + two persons + enclosure
Garden

Reading Pictures

All languages use symbols: signs or pictures that represent real things or ideas. The early Egyptians used drawings to represent words. They could make these drawings on stone or on a scroll. Thousands of miles to the east, the early Chinese developed a system of printed characters that stood for words and ideas. People still use symbols today.

Sometimes symbols make up a rebus, a kind of code containing both words and pictures.

Symbols often serve as a quick way to give directions, rules, or locations.

From Pictures to Letters

Today most of our writing uses words rather than pictures.

For thousands of years, though, from prehistoric cave dwellers to the early Egyptians, pictures were the only kind of writing.

But it's hard to draw a picture of everything that human beings can think about. What does "yesterday" look like, or "cold," or "possible"? Gradually people invented ways to make pictures more abstract: they started to stand for more than just the things people could see or touch.

After many centuries people discovered that they could even turn their pictures into symbols that represented the sounds of their language.

Sumerian Pictograms
3000 B.C.

= day

= hand

= ox

= water

= orchard

Egyptian Hieroglyphics

Indus Valley Seal

These "sound pictures" are called letters, written symbols standing for the sounds that make up all of our words. Every language has thousands and thousands of words, but only a limited number of sounds. So each language needs relatively few letters.

A list, in a particular order, of all the letters used in a language is called an alphabet. No one can be sure just when or where people first put together an alphabet, but the alphabet we use in English today goes all the way back to the ancient Middle East.

Ancient Greek

Get the Picture?

Scientists interested in the history of languages have traced our alphabet back to about 2000 B.C., or 4,000 years ago. These scientists study ancient languages and examine clay tablets and other inscriptions found in ancient ruins. They compare what they find in one place with evidence discovered in other places. They also compare writing from one age with samples from others.

It's often hard to figure out exactly what these ancient pictures meant originally. Examples of ancient writing have been lost over the centuries, so there is much that we do not know for sure. Scholars today are still trying to learn more about the history of our alphabet.

Cuneiform

Egyptian Hieroglyphics

Around the Mediterranean and Through the Centuries

How did an alphabet that got its start some 4,000 years ago become our modern alphabet?

Caravans, commerce, and conquest! Our alphabet developed over many centuries in the lands around the Mediterranean Sea.

The alphabet originally created by the Sinaitic ("living in Sinai") peoples was a major advance in human communication. Easier to learn and use than pictures, the letters worked just as well for Phoenician, Greek, and Latin (the language of the Romans). Later, they turned out to be just as useful for languages as different as English, Spanish, German, Polish, Turkish, and Hawaiian.

Today's English letters probably began as Egyptian picture symbols (1), borrowed by the peoples of the Sinai Peninsula (2) and turned into letters, which were borrowed by the Phoenicians (3), who passed them on to the Greeks (4), who lent them to the Romans (5), who passed them on to us.

ROME AD 100

5

The Romans, from Italy, replaced the Greeks as the most powerful people in the Mediterranean world by about 200 B.C. They soon expanded their empire into Portugal, Spain, France, and other parts of Europe, including Britain. Wherever they went, they took their alphabet, based on the Greek letters, with them.

By 800 B.C. the Greeks had changed the shape of most Phoenician letters and added a few of their own. These letters proved to be quite useful, even though the Greek language was very different from Phoenician. Everywhere that the Greeks established colonies around the Mediterranean, their alphabet was used in government and business.

early Greek 800B.C.

GREECE 4

late Greek 400 B.C.

The Phoenicians, who lived on the Mediterranean coast near Sinai, adapted the Sinaitic alphabet to their own language. Developed between 1000 and 800 B.C., their alphabet had 20 letters. Great shipbuilders and sailors, the Phoenicians bought and sold goods all around the Mediterranean. They soon spread their alphabet to their trading partners, including the Greeks.

PHOENICIA 3

1000 B.C.

1 Just a few years ago, scientists came across some carvings on a rock wall in Egypt's Nile Valley. They believe these 4,000-year-old carvings are letters: symbols that represent sounds, not things or ideas. They are the very first example of an alphabet. They were probably carved not by Egyptians, but by miners or other foreign workers from the nearby Sinai Peninsula.

The Sinaitic peoples traded goods back and forth with Egypt, so they were familiar with Egyptian picture writing, or hieroglyphics. Many of the letters they created, scientists think, are based on Egyptian symbols. By about 1500 B.C. the Sinaitic peoples had developed an alphabet of 18 letters.

SINAI PENINSULA 2

1500 B.C.

EGYPT

2000 B.C.

A

In the ancient Middle East, the ox was an important animal. Oxen plowed fields for grain and cotton and turned waterwheels to irrigate the fields. Oxen provided meat, as well as hides for clothing and tents.

The early Semitic name for this useful animal, *aleph*, became the first letter of the Sinaitic alphabet. Originally this letter looked like an ox head. Turned upside down, our modern A still shows the horns of an ox!

When the Greeks borrowed this letter, they called it *alpha*.

SINAITIC   PHOENICIAN   EARLY GREEK   CLASSICAL GREEK   ROMAN

But What Did It Sound Like?

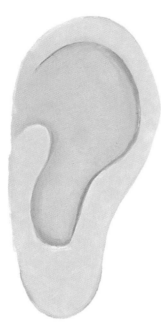

We can't be sure about the exact sounds the letters of early alphabets represented. Scientists believe *aleph* was a kind of throaty *h* sound that doesn't exist in English.

We do know that *aleph* was a consonant, not a vowel as A is in English. Consonants are sounds made by stopping or restricting the flow of air as we speak. Vowel sounds are made without interfering with the flow of air.

Semitic languages such as ancient Sinaitic and Phoenician or modern Hebrew and Arabic are written without vowel letters. All the letters of these alphabets are consonants. Vowels are pronounced in speaking but are not used in writing.

From the sense of the sentence, Semitic peoples can tell which vowels are missing. For example, if we wrote in English, "Th bg dg brkd" we could probably figure out that the missing vowels are E, I, O, A, and E ("The big dog barked").

At first glance B may not look like a good place to live, but that's what it was originally: a house or home, *beth* to the peoples of the Middle East.

The ancient word *beth* shows up in some modern place-names. Bethlehem (a city in Pennsylvania) means "house of bread," while Bethesda (a city in Maryland) is "merciful house," and Bethel (a town in Connecticut) is "house of God."

The Sinaitic letter probably represents the floor plan of a simple one-room house.

The Phoenicians made theirs with a point at the top, perhaps indicating a tent.

The Greeks at first made their letter with two points and called it *beta*.

Later they began to round off the points to form the letter we use today.

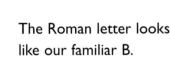

The Roman letter looks like our familiar B.

Who Named It the "Alphabet?"

Our word *alphabet* comes from the first two Greek letters, *alpha* and *beta*. The Greeks didn't invent the idea of an alphabet, but they did give us the word for it.

The Romans originally called their list of letters *literae*, "letters," or *elementa*, "elements," a word that may have come from the "L-M-N" sequence in the middle of the list. By about the third century B.C., however, they were using the word *alphabetum*, from the first two Greek letters, which became our word *alphabet*.

C G

In the world of letters, G is a close relative of C. In fact, C started off in Sinaitic and Phoenician times as a way of writing a *g* sound.

C began as the letter *gimel*. Some linguists believe it came from a word meaning "throwing stick," a tool used for hunting animals. Many others trace it to the word for "camel." The Phoenician form may represent the camel's hump. Still others, looking at the Sinaitic form, suggest that the word meant "corner."

When the Greeks borrowed this letter, they named it *gamma* and used it for their g sound. The Romans added a stroke at the bottom and rounded off the letter. Originally they used it for both their g sound and k sound. (We can't be sure, after all these years, just why they did this, since the Greek alphabet had a letter for the k sound.)

The new letter had a form very much like a C, but with a small crossbar so the two would not be confused.

corner
GimeL

14

SinAiTiC   PHOENICIA

It's Just a Name

The Greeks were the first people to use letter names that had no other meaning. To the Phoenicians, *aleph* was both a letter and a word—in this case, one meaning "ox." *Beth* was a letter and a word meaning "house," *gimel*, a letter and a word referring to a kind of stick. *Alpha*, *beta*, and *gamma*, however, were just letters to the Greeks, representing sounds in their language. These letter names had no other meaning. The Greeks had moved all the way from picture writing to a true alphabet.

A *alpha*

B *beta*

Γ *gamma*

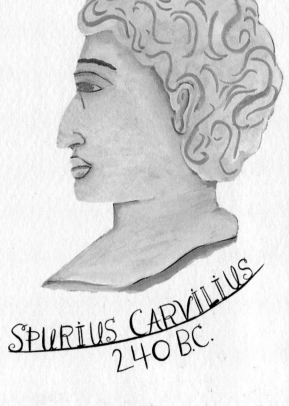

SPURIUS CARVILIUS
240 B.C.

One Roman writer tells us that it was a teacher and former slave named Spurius Carvilius who actually suggested putting the letter G in the alphabet around 240 B.C., though no one can be certain.

Γ   C   G

EARLY GREEK   CLASSICAL GREEK   ROMAN

Scientists are fairly certain that our D began as the Phoenician letter *daleth*, meaning "door." What they are not sure about is where this letter came from and why it looks so little like a door!

Some people feel that the Phoenician character looks like a carved panel on a wooden door. Others think that it represents a flap of animal skin covering the opening to a tent.

Another idea is that the shape of *daleth* came from a different Sinaitic letter, *dag*, which may have meant a kind of fish. Perhaps, the theory goes, the Phoenician letter is just the head of the older Sinaitic fish. After almost 4,000 years, it's hard to tell for sure.

PHOENICIAN

EARLY GREEK

CLASSICAL GREEK

ROMAN

16

Wherever it came from originally, the Greeks turned the Phoenician door into a neat triangle and called it *delta*. We use this word to mean the triangular piece of land formed by silt at the mouth of a river. In a sense, the delta is like the doorway to the river.

Now I Know My ABCs

The Romans were the first people to name their letters by the sounds they represent, as we do today in English: *ay, bee, cee, dee, ee, eff, gee,* and so on.

The Greeks, on the other hand, still used letter names that recalled the older Phoenician and Sinaitic picture words, such as *alpha, beta, gamma,* and *delta.*

The origin of the letter E is uncertain. The Sinaitic symbol for the word *he* looks a bit like a person with upstretched arms, and perhaps it indicated someone praying. Or it may instead have meant "high." Most scholars today believe that the drawing simply represented a person expressing surprise.

The Phoenician symbol for *he* looks entirely different, and some believe it meant "window." Whatever its meaning, it was a consonant in both Sinaitic and Phoenician.

Borrowed by the Greeks, this letter became a vowel called *epsilon*. In Greek, *psilon* means "plain" or "simple." So *epsilon*—(h)*e-psilon*—was their plain, or short *e*, vowel. They used a different letter for their long *e* sound.

1800 B.C.

Semitic letter "he" represents a person's shout of surprise

SINAITIC   PHOENICIAN   EARLY GREEK   CLASSICAL GREEK   ROMAN

And That's an Order

No one knows why the letters of the alphabet appear in the order they do. They've kept pretty much the same order since Phoenician times.

Alphabetical order helps us to organize information. A dictionary that just listed thousands of words in no particular order would be almost impossible to use.

At the Olympic Games, Greece (home of the first Olympics) always enters the arena first, and the host nation's team is always last. In between, though, the rest of the teams enter in . . . you guessed it, alphabetical order!

The alphabetical order at the Olympics is in the language of the host country. The United States enters toward the end, following the United Kingdom, as long as the games are held in an English-speaking country. When the games are held in a French- or Spanish-speaking country, however, the United States enters much earlier, under the E's for *États-Unis* in French or *Estados Unidos* in Spanish.

F
U
V
W
Y

Five of our letters, F, U, V, W, and Y, all come from one picture letter, *vau*, used by the Sinaitic people. Some very interesting things happened to *vau* during its travels through the centuries.

On the Sinai Peninsula, the consonant *vau* was written with a curved top and probably had a *v* sound.

The Phoenicians changed the top of the letter, called it *waw*, and pronounced it, we think, with a *w* sound.

The Greeks turned this letter into two separate letters in their alphabet.

By twisting the top and then turning the letter around, the Greeks created *digamma*. This was a consonant, standing for the *w* sound. The sound was so rare in Greek words that the letter was hardly used. The Greeks finally dropped it from their alphabet.

Rounding the top of the Phoenician letter, the Greeks also created a vowel letter, *upsilon*, which represented a *u* sound.

SINAITIC

PHOENICIAN

or

EARLY GREEK 800BC.

CLASSICAL GREEK

20

The Romans borrowed both *digamma* and *upsilon*. *Digamma* they kept as a consonant, but they used it for their *f* sound. Today in English, it has this same sound.

The Romans cut off *upsilon*'s stem and sharpened its top into an angle. They used this letter as both a consonant, with a *w* sound, and as a vowel with a *u* sound.

After several centuries, the Romans began to write this letter with a rounded bottom. It was easier to carve V into stone, but much easier to write U in ink on parchment. So, for centuries, people switched back and forth between the V form and the U form. By the 1700s, people in England had started to use V only as a consonant and U only as a vowel.

The *w* sound of modern English was written, in the Middle Ages, as UU ("double U.") By the 1500s it was the style to write the letter as W (actually "double V"), which is what we do today.

The Romans also kept the original Greek *upsilon*, again sharpening the angle at the top, and used it only in words they took directly from Greek. It probably had a kind of *i* sound, and was often confused with the letter I. Today English uses Y as a consonant in words such as *yet* or *you* and as a vowel in words such as *baby* or *my*.

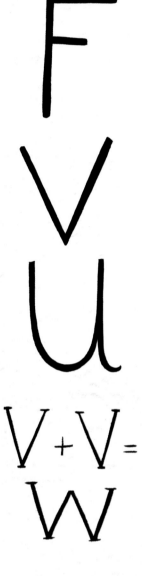

21

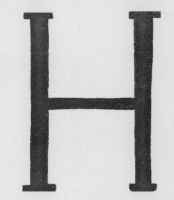

H

H started out as a consonant, turned into a vowel, and is now a consonant again.

Kheth meant "braid" or "twisted rope" in the Sinaitic languages. It was a consonant, pronounced with a kind of *h* sound.

The Phoenicians changed the symbol for *kheth*; to them, *kheth* meant "fence" (though it may look more like a ladder to us), but it was still a consonant with the *h* sound.

The Greeks closed up the fence, called the letter *eta*, and used it as a vowel, their long *e*.

The Romans, who used E for both long *e* and short *e*, now had a letter (*eta*) left over from the Greeks. This was convenient, because they had an *h* sound and needed a letter for it. So they borrowed *eta* and changed its form to make the consonant H.

Sinaitic

Phoenician
"Kheth"=fence

early Greek
heta or eta

Classical Greek H

Roman H

Turning Consonants into Vowels

Languages do not all share exactly the same sounds. A sound used in one language may not exist in another. Sounds that seem very different to speakers of one language may sound alike to a speaker of another language.

For example, the Sinaitic and Phoenician sounds of *aleph, he,* and *kheth* all sounded very different to speakers of those languages, but would sound the same to us, because only one of those sounds exists in English. To Germans, who have no *w* sound, our English V and W sound alike.

The Greeks, who wanted a letter for each sound in a word, didn't need some of the Phoenician consonants, because the sounds they represented were not used in Greek. So they took Phoenician consonants like *aleph, he,* and *kheth* and used them for the vowel sounds they called *alpha, epsilon,* and *eta.*

In many languages today, there are far more sounds than letters. The English alphabet has 26 letters, but depending on their accent, most English speakers use more than 40 different sounds! Many of our letters represent more than one sound, such as the O in *pot, to,* and *open.*

I
J

Like C and G, the letters I and J are closely related. Both come from *yod*, the Sinaitic and Phoenician word for "arm" or "hand." You can almost see the fingers of a hand in the ancient letterforms.

Yod began as a consonant, probably like the first sound in *yard*. The Greeks called it *iota* and gave it a simpler form. This was another Phoenician consonant the Greeks didn't need, so they used it as the vowel I.

The Romans used this letter for two distinct sounds. One was a vowel sound, probably like the *i* of *machine*, while the other was a consonant similar to the *y* in *yet*.

By the Middle Ages, people began to pronounce the consonant sound more like the *j* in *jet* than the *y* in *yet*.

Around the sixteenth century A.D., people started writing a little hook at the bottom of the letter when it was used to represent a consonant.

That's how our modern J was born. The form without the hook became I in English.

SINAITIC   PHOENICIAN   EARLY GREEK   CLASSICAL GREEK   ROMAN

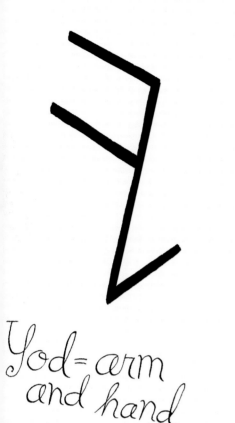

Yod = arm and hand

But It Doesn't Sound the Same!

Many languages use the same letters, but often with different sounds. For example, English, Spanish, and German all use J.

In English we call this letter *jay* after the sound it stands for.

The Spanish J is called *jota* and stands for an *h* sound.

In German it's called *Jot* and has a *y* sound. Same letter, different languages, different sounds. People are very good at making the same alphabet fit the sounds of their own languages.

K
Q

The Sinaitic and Phoenician alphabets both had letters for two kinds of *k* sounds. Although the sounds were similar, the letters were very different.

One of those *k*-sound letters was called *kaph*, meaning "the palm of the hand," which gave us our K. The other letter was called *qoph*, from which we got our Q. Scholars are not sure just what the *qoph* drawing represented. Maybe it was a knot in a rope, or possibly a monkey or an ape, or even the eye of a needle.

The Greeks borrowed *kaph*, called it *kappa*, and gave it the K form it has today. The Romans borrowed it from them, and though they rarely used it themselves (because their C had the same *k* sound) they passed it on to us.

In some parts of Greece, people also used *qoph*, calling it *koppa*. The Romans also borrowed this letter, forming it as Q. They used it only before a U, as we do in words like *quart*, *queen*, *quiet*, and *quota*.

SINAITIC

PHOENICIAN

EARLY GREEK

CLASSICAL GREEK

ROMAN

"Kaph"

Today Rome, Tomorrow the World!

The most widely used alphabet around the world today is the one the Romans used centuries ago. As Roman armies conquered the rest of Europe, people in Spain, France, Italy, Germany, Scandinavia, and England began to write their languages in the alphabet of Rome. These same countries spread their cultures in colonies of their own in Asia, Africa, and the Americas, so people on those continents also use the Roman alphabet.

Since most languages have more sounds than letters, people found a number of ways to use existing letters to represent several different sounds. English, for example, sometimes combines letters such as *CH, SH,* and *TH*. Spanish *RR* is different from R, and *LL* different from L.

Besides the Roman, other widely used alphabets of similar origins are the Hebrew and Arabic, which are based on the Phoenician, and the Cyrillic, used in Russia and Eastern Europe, which came from the Greek alphabet.

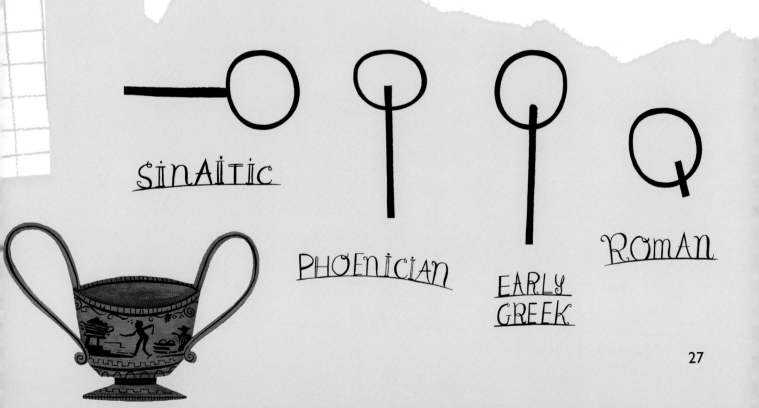

SINAITIC

PHOENICIAN

EARLY GREEK

ROMAN

L

In a sense, the letter L is connected to the letter A.

Aleph, or A, was the ox. To get their oxen going, the peoples of Sinai used a special cattle prod called a *lamed*. The symbol for this useful stick became our letter L.

SINAITIC

The Phoenicians turned the stick upside down.

PHOENICIAN

The Greeks first gave the stick a sharp angle. Later they flipped the angle up and straightened out the sides.

EARLY GREEK

CLASSICAL GREEK

The Romans turned it over again, giving us our modern L.

28 ROMAN

Back and Forth and Back Again

Today most languages are read from left to right. But the most ancient
Greeks sometimes wrote in both directions, something like this:
First they wrote from left to right, and whenever they came to the end of
the line they simply went back the way they had come going in the other
direction, back and forth from left to right and right to left. It must have
been easier for them than for us to read.

The Greeks had to learn all their letters backward and forward! This form
of writing is called "boustrophedon," which means "as the ox plows"—
turning at the end of a row to go back the other way.

M

When you hear someone say "water," you might think of drinking, bathing, washing, swimming, or cooking.

How about the letter M? Most of us don't think about M in connection with water, but that is exactly where this letter came from. Can you see why M, in its original Sinaitic form, would mean "water"?

The Sinai peoples and the Phoenicians both called this letter *mem*, their word for water. In both letterforms, you can still see the waves! The Phoenicians in particular were great shipbuilders and sailors. No wonder they used a water symbol in their alphabet.

SINAITIC

PHOENICIAN

EARLY GREEK

CLASSICAL GREEK

ROMAN

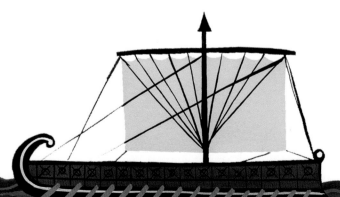

Spacing Out

It isn't always easy for us to read Roman writing,

BECAUSETHEYUSEDONLYCAPITALLETTERSANDD
IDNTHAVEANYPUNCTUATIONMARKSTHEYALSO
WROTEWITHOUTANYSPACESBETWEENTHEWOR
DSORSENTENCESANDJUSTRANEVERYTHINGTOG
ETHERLIKETHISWHENTHEYRANOUTOFSPACEAT
THEENDOFALINETHEYJUSTDIVIDEDWORDSBET
WEENLETTERS

After a while even the Romans got tired of reading like
this, so they began to put spaces between words and a
dot like this • between sentences. That dot became the
punctuation mark we call a period.

THIS IS EASIER TO READ • THE ROMANS
STILL USED ONLY CAPITAL LETTERS •

It's even easier to read when the more familiar lowercase
letters are used.

N

Looking at the Sinaitic symbol for the word *nun*, what would you think it means?

A snake? A fish? A flash of lightning?

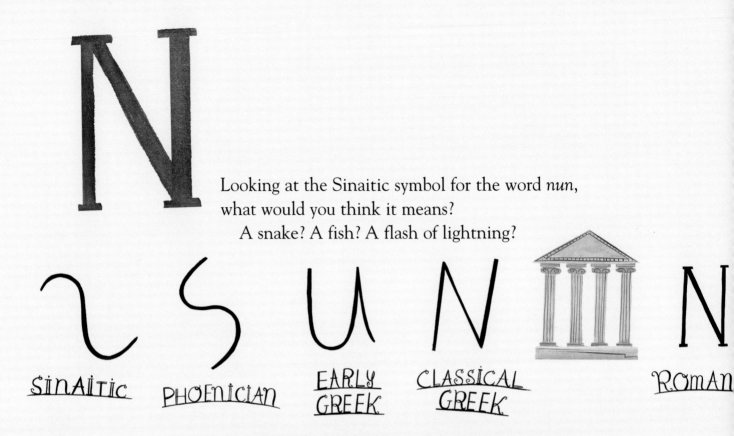

SINAITIC   PHOENICIAN   EARLY GREEK   CLASSICAL GREEK   ROMAN

Living along the shores of the Red Sea and the Mediterranean, the peoples of Sinai and Phoenicia certainly relied on fish for a large part of their diets. Scientists think that the Phoenician letter, which looks more like a fish, or at least a fish head, than the Sinaitic form, represents the word *nun*, "fish" in both Sinaitic and Phoenician.

It's possible, though, that the Sinaitic letter was not a fish at all, but a snake, *namesh*, and that the Phoenicians turned it into a fish shape to make it look more like their M letter, *mem*.

Perhaps over the centuries the letter came to look more like a fish because of the close relationship of M and N in the alphabet. The two letters stand next to each other, and both are nasal sounds, pronounced by passing air through the nose. In fact, in English these are two of just three nasal sounds (the other is the *ng* sound of *ring*). And the Phoenician words *mem* and *nun* are both related to the sea ("water" and "fish"), which is another way that M and N seem to be similar.

N = fish

32

Write On!

The Egyptians invented a material called papyrus that was made from a plant that grew along the Nile River. Its surface was highly suited to drawing. Papyrus was very expensive, so people wrote on both sides of a sheet. They also developed inks that could be washed off so the papyrus could be reused.

The peoples of Sinai and Phoenicia did their earliest writing on clay tablets. It's hard to draw clearly detailed pictures in soft clay, which may be one reason why alphabets developed in this region.

The Greeks and Romans used both papyrus scrolls and clay tablets. They often carved inscriptions into the stone of their public buildings, too. Many Romans carried with them small wax-covered wooden boards to write on. Just by warming the wax with their hands, Romans could "wipe the slate clean" and start over.

By the Middle Ages, people were writing on specially prepared animal skins called parchment. The finest parchment was known as vellum. Both these materials were extremely expensive, limiting the amount of writing that was done.

Paper, invented in China during the first century A.D., did not reach Western Europe until the twelfth century. Until methods for mass production were invented centuries later, paper remained a luxury to be enjoyed by only a wealthy few.

Egyptian

𓂋 = Scribe

Black ink was made of soot and papyrus juice.

Papyrus Plant

O P R S

The peoples of Sinai and Phoenicia derived their letters from drawings of everyday objects. Four of our letters—O, P, R, and S—came from their words for parts of the head.

P○ ○ ○ ○ ○
SINAITIC   PHOENICIAN   EARLY GREEK   CLASSICAL GREEK   ROMAN

ayin

O comes from *ayin*, the word for "eye." When the Greeks borrowed this letter, they made it rounder and turned this consonant into a vowel that they named *omicron*.

Pe, "mouth," gave us the letter P. At first the Greek letter looked a lot like the Phoenician form of the word. The Romans borrowed that form, writing it as P, the letter we use today.

Pe

SINAITIC   PHOENICIAN   EARLY GREEK   CLASSICAL GREEK   ROMAN

P P P P R

R came to us from *resh*, a word meaning "head." The Greeks called this letter *rho*, and wrote it as P. The Romans added the tail that gave us our modern R.

With a head (R) and a mouth (P), you have room for a set of teeth. And that's where S comes in. *Shin* was most likely the Sinaitic word for "teeth." In Phoenician, *shin* had a *sh* sound, but the Greeks used it for their *s* sound. They also turned it on its side. The Romans rounded off the points to make our familiar S.

W W W 3 Σ S

SINAITIC   PHOENICIAN   EARLY GREEK   CLASSICAL GREEK   ROMAN

W = tooth

35

When the letter T got its start, it looked more like an X.

It began life as the Sinaitic letter *tau*. Possibly this symbol represented the spokes on a wheel. More likely it was a word meaning "mark" or "sign." Even today, people who have not learned to write use a very similar mark to sign important papers.

The Phoenician letter looks almost exactly like the Sinaitic one. The Greeks moved the cross-stroke up to the top of the letter. This was the only letter whose name the Greeks did not change. *Aleph* became *alpha*, *beth* became *beta*, and so on, but *tau* remained *tau*.

The Romans passed on the Greek letter without any changes, so our modern T looks as it did in the days of the Greeks.

Signature

SINAITIC   PHOENICIAN   EARLY GREEK   CLASSICAL GREEK   ROMAN

It's a Matter of Style

The Romans often carved messages in stone. They found that adding a short cross-stroke at the ends of most letters helped to finish off the form of carved letters more neatly.

A H T V S

This cross-stroke is called a *serif*, which means "line" in French.

In modern times, as printing evolved and new typefaces, or fonts, were designed, people often wanted a simpler look. Some fonts eliminate the cross-strokes. These fonts are called *sans serif*, from the French for "without a line."

A H T V S

Sometimes when we want to set words or sentences apart, we put them in italic type.

In italic fonts, the printed letters all slant to the right, like this.
This kind of typeface was invented in Italy during the Middle Ages.

Another way to emphasize a word is to print it in boldface.
Boldface fonts are heavier and darker than regular printed letters.

With the invention of printing, more people learned to read and to write. Carefully printing each letter takes time, so people developed what we call cursive writing.

Cursive writing is also called script and looks something like this.
In cursive writing, the shapes of letters are changed so that they can be linked together and the pen or pencil does not have to stop or lift off the paper as often as it does with printing.

37

X goes all the way back to the days of the Sinaitic and Phoenician peoples, but got to us through some confusion in both Greek and Roman times.

The Phoenician alphabet had a letter *shin* (a *sh* sound) and a letter *samekh* (an *s* sound). The original Sinaitic letter *samekh* may have meant "fish" or "fishbone." In Phoenician it was probably a "pillar" or "support post."

The Greeks, as we've seen, borrowed *shin* for their *s* sound, and it became the ancestor of our modern S. They also had a *ks* sound (like the sound in our word *books*) that needed a letter, and for this they used *samekh*, changing its sound from *s* to *ks*. The Greek letter, called *xi*, still looked much like the Phoenician letter.

But some Greeks, especially in very early times, wrote this letter as X instead. The Romans borrowed the X form, and this is the way it has come down to us, giving us the *ks* sound of *box* or *exit*.

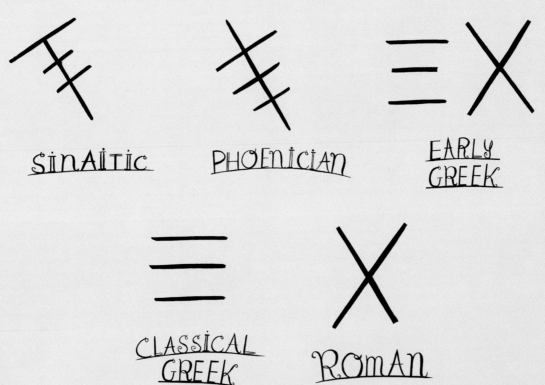

SINAITIC   PHOENICIAN   EARLY GREEK

CLASSICAL GREEK   ROMAN

Getting into Print

Until Johannes Gutenberg came along in the mid-1400s, writing was done by hand. Gutenberg made two important innovations. One was the invention of movable type, where each letter was cast from a small piece of metal. The other was the printing press, which meant that hundreds of copies of a book could be produced almost as easily as a single copy.

Printing and typesetting changed very little until the late 19th century, when machines were invented that could set an entire line or even a page of type automatically. In the 20th century, printing advanced so much that today entire books, both type and art, are composed on a computer and printed on huge automated presses—just like this one was!

Gutenberg Press

Z is the only letter that was once thrown out of the alphabet and later allowed back in.

To the Sinai peoples and the Phoenicians, *zayin* meant "weapon" or "dagger." The Greeks called this letter *zeta* and changed its form, connecting the top and bottom with a diagonal stroke.

The Romans never really used the Greek *zeta*. They had no words that used the *z* sound, except a few that were Greek anyway, so they decided that S was close enough for those words. In 312 B.C. an official named Caecus ordered Z removed from the alphabet. It had originally appeared after F, and G was inserted in its place a few years later.

By around 100 A.D. the Romans were borrowing more and more Greek words. They found that Z would be a useful letter after all. They added it to the end of the alphabet, where it remains today.

Zee

U.S.A.

↓ Ι Ι Ζ Ζ

SINAITIC PHOENICIAN EARLY GREEK CLASSICAL GREEK ROMAN

That's What I Zed!

Z is the only letter of the alphabet that has a different name in the United States and Britain. Although it represents the same sound on both sides of the Atlantic, we call it "zee," while the British call it "zed."

So now we've explored the alphabet from A to Z, or as the British would say, from A to Zed.

A Gift From Ancient Times

Alphabets are used all over the world. By some estimates, more than three-quarters of the world's languages use alphabets, and about sixty percent of the world's population speaks languages that have a written alphabet.

Of course, millions of people, mostly in Asia, speak languages whose written forms use picture symbols, called *logograms* ("word-writing") or *ideograms* ("idea-writing").

Many of the languages of India use an alphabet system called *Devanagari*. The symbols appear very different from our Roman alphabet. There is enough similarity, though, in some of the forms that scientists believe this alphabet, too, came at least in part from the Phoenician writing system.

Elsewhere in the world, the Roman alphabet dominates. Developed originally by the Sinaitic peoples, adapted by the Phoenicians and the Greeks, and passed on to us through a long history of trade, conquest, and borrowing, the Roman alphabet serves dozens of the world's languages.

Even those languages that use non-Roman letterforms show some similarity to the English alphabet and show that they are all originally a gift from the ancient peoples of the Middle East.

What advantages does an alphabet have?

For one thing, it's a simple system to learn. To read English, we need to learn the shapes of only twenty-six letters. For reading Chinese, you need to know several hundred different characters! It's also easier to write or print letters than to draw individual pictures.

In our electronic age our computer keyboards are much simpler, easier, and faster to use than they would be if each idea had to be represented by a separate symbol and a separate key.

The alphabet created so long ago in the Middle East still serves us remarkably well today, making communication an easy and efficient task.

Here are the first two letter symbols and their names in several languages. The forms may look different, but the names certainly have a familiar ring!

					Language
𐤀	aleph	⌂	beth		Sinaitic
⪦	aleph	⪤	bayt		Phoenician
Λ	alpha	Β	beta		Greek
A	ay	B	bee		Roman
א	aleph	ב	veth		Hebrew
ا	alif	ب	be		Arabic
А	ah	Б	beh		Russian

Cast of Characters

The study of ancient languages is a science. As in all sciences, new discoveries may lead to new conclusions. Scientists may disagree about the meanings of symbols that are more than three thousand years old. The chart below summarizes both things that are fairly certain and things that are still under investigation.

Letter	Probable Source	Approximate First Use	Possible Meaning(s)
A	Sinai	1500 B.C.	ox
B	Sinai	1500 B.C.	house
C	Sinai	1500 B.C.	stick or camel or corner
D	Phoenicia	1000 B.C.	door
E	Sinai	1500 B.C.	surprise or prayer or high
F	Sinai	1500 B.C.	hook or nail
G	Rome	A.D. 250	
H	Sinai	A.D. 1500	braid or twisted rope
I	Sinai	A.D. 1500	arm or hand
J	England	A.D. 1500–1600	
K	Sinai	1500 B.C.	palm of hand
L	Sinai	1500 B.C.	prod
M	Sinai	1500 B.C.	water
N	Sinai	1500 B.C.	fish or snake
O	Sinai	1500 B.C.	eye
P	Sinai	1500 B.C.	mouth
Q	Sinai	1500 B.C.	knot or monkey
R	Sinai	1500 B.C.	head

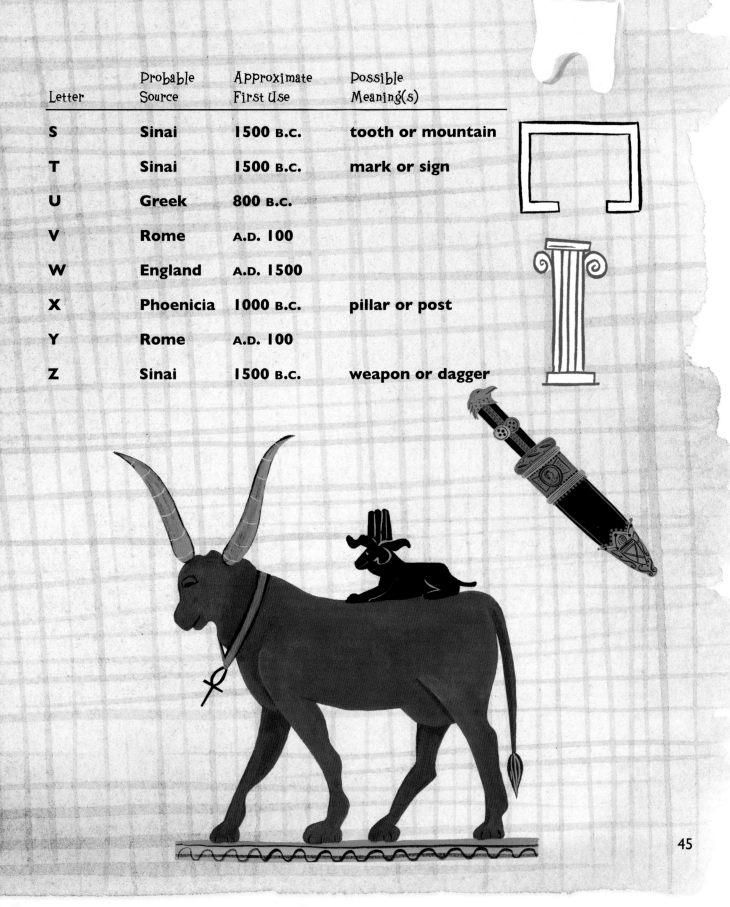

Letter	Probable Source	Approximate First Use	Possible Meaning(s)
S	Sinai	1500 B.C.	tooth or mountain
T	Sinai	1500 B.C.	mark or sign
U	Greek	800 B.C.	
V	Rome	A.D. 100	
W	England	A.D. 1500	
X	Phoenicia	1000 B.C.	pillar or post
Y	Rome	A.D. 100	
Z	Sinai	1500 B.C.	weapon or dagger

Resources

Books for Children

Dugan, William. *How Our Alphabet Grew: The History of the Alphabet*. Houston: Golden Press, 1972.

Fisher, Leonard Everett. *Alphabet Art: Thirteen ABCs from Around the World*. New York: Four Winds Press, 1978.

Ogg, Oscar. *The 26 Letters*. New York: Thomas Y. Crowell, 1948.

Rees, Ennis. *The Little Greek Alphabet Book*. Englewood Cliffs, NJ: Prentice Hall, 1968.

Samoyault, Tiphaine. *Alphabetical Order: How the Alphabet Began*. New York: Viking, 1998.

Websites

Ancient Scripts: Alphabet
http://www.ancientscripts.com/alphabet.html

Greatest Inventions: The Alphabet
http://www.edinformatics.com/inventions_inventors/alphabet.htm

The History of Writing
http://www.historian.net/hxwrite.htm

Books for Adults

Firmage, Richard A. *The Alphabet Abecedarium: Some Notes on Letters*. Boston: David R. Godine, 1993.

Haley, Allan. *Alphabet: The History, Evolution, and Design of the Letters We Use Today*. London: Thames and Hudson, 1995.

Jean, Georges. *Writing: The Story of Alphabets and Scripts*. New York: Harry N. Abrams, 1992.

Ouaknin, Mark-Alain. *Mysteries of the Alphabet: The Origins of Writing*. New York: Abbeville Press, 1999.

Sacks, David. *Language Visible: Unraveling the Mystery of the Alphabet from A to Z*. New York: Broadway Books/Random House, 2003.

To Maura, who has always had a gift for language—D. R.

To J. C. A. with love—A. S.

Special thanks to Dr. Joshua T. Katz of Princeton University for his
expertise and advice.

Text copyright © 2007 by Donald Robb
Illustrations copyright © 2007 by Anne Smith/Lilla Rogers Studio
All rights reserved, including the right of reproduction in whole or in part
in any form. Charlesbridge and colophon are registered trademarks of
Charlesbridge Publishing, Inc.

Published by Charlesbridge
85 Main Street
Watertown, MA 02472
(617) 926-0329
www.charlesbridge.com

Library of Congress Cataloging-in-Publication Data
Robb, Don.
    Ox, house, stick : the history of our alphabet / Donald Robb ; illustrated
by Anne Smith.
       p. cm.
    ISBN 978-1-57091-609-0 (reinforced for library use)
    ISBN 978-1-57091-610-6 (softcover)
1. English language—Alphabet—Juvenile literature. I. Smith, Anne,
1958– II. Title.
PE1155.R615 2005
428.1'3—dc22   2005006015

Printed in China
(hc) 10 9 8 7 6 5 4 3 2
(sc) 10 9 8 7 6 5 4 3 2 1

Illustrations painted in gouache
Display type and text type set in Goudy, Flora Dora, and Gill Sans
Printed and bound by Jade Productions
Production supervision by Brian G. Walker
Designed by Susan Mallory Sherman

J 428.1 ROBB $16.95
Robb, Don.
Ox, house, stick :
48 p. :

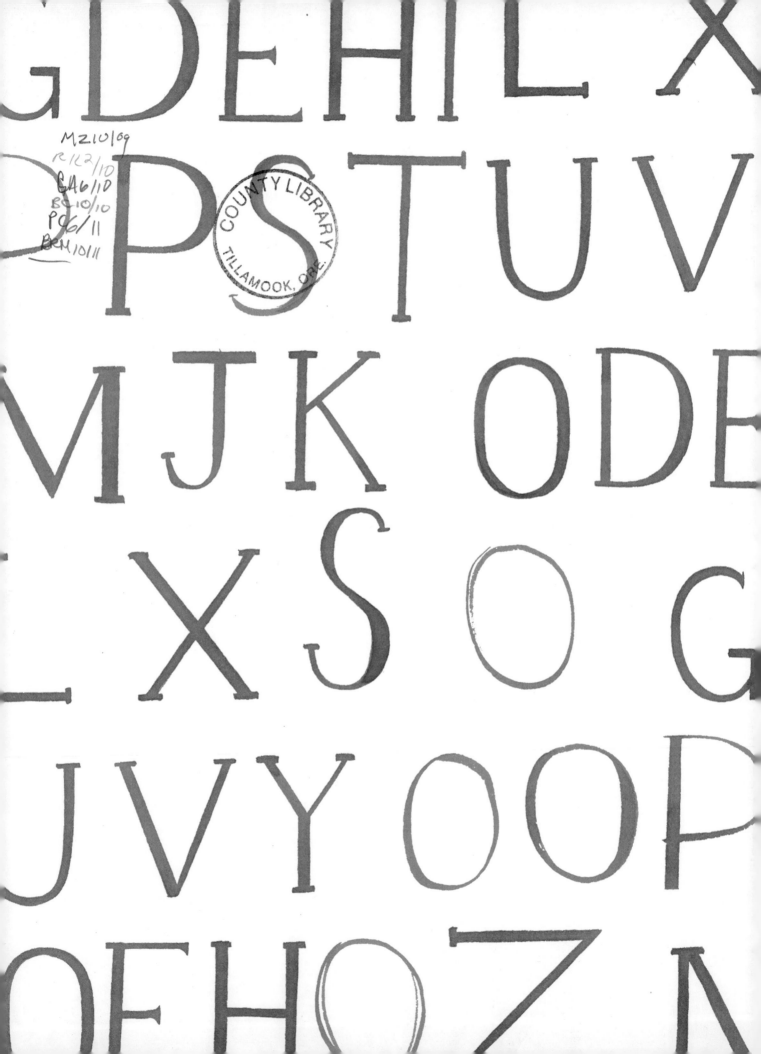
MZ10/09
R12/10
GA6/10
BC10/10
PC6/11
BM10/11

COUNTY LIBRARY
TILLAMOOK, ORE.